Log of Judgments

Arch-Preacher John Wesley Ellis I

authorHOUSE®

AuthorHouse™
1663 Liberty Drive, Suite 200
Bloomington, IN 47403
www.authorhouse.com
Phone: 1-800-839-8640

First published by AuthorHouse 2/5/2008

ISBN: 978-1-4343-4768-8 (e)
ISBN: 978-1-4343-4766-4 (sc)
ISBN: 978-1-4343-4767-1 (hc)

Library of Congress Control Number: 2007908852

Printed in the United States of America
Bloomington, Indiana

This book is printed on acid-free paper.

Table of Contents

INTRODUCTION

I will begin this introduction with a simple question, how can I help a nation that will not listen to the revealed Truth from God? How can I pray for an apostatized nation that refuses to repent of so many actable and noticeable evil ways? The prophesied Judgments of Elohim upon this world are imminent and will be fulfilled. The beginning of these judgments, which were spoken of by the prophets, are about to be manifested on a great, phenomenal scale. The people in this world have experienced many catastrophic events before, but not of this magnitude since the Great Flood in the days of Noah.

Everything in existence obeys the voice of Elohim. It is the written and preached Word of God that men and women have refused to obey and accept. Because of the epidemic of manifested pride, the great judgments upon this world are about to begin. Why should there be the judgments of God's great wrath upon the people before they will listen and be humbled into obedience? The knowledge of the past historical events reveals a trend of evil, then destruction, and the results of repentance. The future historical events reveal a different trend, which is the destruction of evil and eternal salvation for the repented people of God. Are hurricanes, tornadoes, earthquakes, tsunamis, diseases, famines, wars, volcanoes, and many other means of speech from Elohim coincidental? Is this what you call Mother Nature? I challenge you in the truth contestation in one of the chapters of this book.

A pound of prevention is better than a pound of cure. The evidence of the past has proven to be insignificant to the present. If Noah was here in the flesh, and fully detailed what happened to cause Elohim to send the Great Flood, you would not listen! It is very obvious and notable that the pleasures of death are more accepted than the Gift of Life through Jesus Christ, our Lord. Satan is a two-faced deceiver.

The time has come for these judgments to be fulfilled. The people are now abusing, without fear, God's wonderfully made creation. How wise are you in thinking that the path of the present has no effect on the future. The poison of greed is everywhere. There is no mercy, in the hearts of many people, for the next generation. Since sin now dominates the world, the implementation of these judgments must take place for eternal restoration. If the evil is not stopped, Satan will cause man to destroy himself.

An all-out nuclear catastrophic event will never be imminent upon the earth that the omnipotent Elohim has created. It will be preserved. It is impossible to change the prophecies. All of the weapons, wisdom, and knowledge that man has cannot change one letter of one word of the declared prophecies of the prophets that spoke as they were moved by the Holy Ghost. Be it well known that man does not own one nucleus of one atom. You should understand that you are in great trouble for helping Satan to attempt to destroy the earth.

CHAPTER ONE:
FULFILLED AND TO BE FULFILLED

There was a day in Eternity of past understanding and finding out that Elohim decided to create and make this world that we now live in. There was no one present to declare, through prophecies, when Elohim was going to fulfill his own desires. No one was present to declare what he was going to make, how he was going to make it, and where he was going to put it. Our great and omnipotent God can declare and fulfill anything that he so desires. There will never be anyone in existence that can tell him what he cannot do or what he must do.

The blinded scientists have determined that substances can create themselves. They have concluded that all of this happened by coincidence. Mathematically speaking, how can you take nothing, add it to nothing, and make something? I have an experiment that I want you to try. Find yourself a large, clear, glass jar with a top that you can certifiably seal. Sterilize the inside of it thoroughly, remove the air, and seal the jar. Make yourself a label that reads, "FOOL'S JAR" and put it on the jar. Tell me in the future how long it took you to realize that the only way that something was going to exist in that jar was if you took the top off and put it in the jar. If the nothing in that jar begins to create something, please find me immediately! I would help you to establish the First Incorporation of Nothing to Something. We would first try to figure out how we could use the jar to make another world with a few changes. If the nothing in the jar remains empty, you must sign your name on the label and become a part of the Holy Scriptures.

How accurate and precise are the prophets and their writings? After God made man, he established a unique and miraculous means of communication. Dreams and visions are an extraordinary means to reveal the Word of God to special chosen men and women. He also ordained an even greater means of communication, which is done by the moving of the Holy Ghost upon a person. Even greater is the face-to-face communication that took place between Elohim and Moses. The greatest communication with man was through his only begotten son, Jesus Christ of Nazareth. Even though the word *prediction* exists, God does not predict that something will happen; neither is prediction used by the prophets. Predictions are based on observations, experience, and scientific reasoning. The attribute of being omniscient would not apply to Elohim if he used predictions.

You sinned before God before you were born. You sinned and repented before God before you were born. Everything that you have done or will do in this life, and in the life to come, you did it before God before you were born. Your thoughts are, in essence, secondhand thoughts. The words of your tongue and your inner tongue are before the Lord God Almighty before you utter them. Because Elohim is omnipotent, omniscient, and omnipresent, he can declare the absolute truth to whomsoever he will.

Are the judgments real and will they be implemented? If you have never been in a great catastrophic event, then doubts will lay upon your intuitional mind. However, if you have personally experienced a great catastrophe, no one will be able to convince you that judgments are not real. Oh wicked and perverse generation, how long will God's Great Grace watch over you? Was the Great Flood a coincidence? Did Noah decide to build an ark for pleasure, or did he by faith obey God and save his life and those that were with him? God did not tell me to build an ark, because Jesus Christ of Nazareth is our complete salvation and refuge.

In a very short unrevealed time, Elohim is going to send his only begotten son upon the earth. I want the world to know this. I also want Satan and the destruction demons to know that when that day comes, their evil works will cease for one thousand years. The Antichrist and the false prophet will be taken and cast alive into the lake of fire and brimstone.

The words that are now being delivered unto you were given to me before I was born that I may be a witness against this evil-minded generation. Elohim has risen up a voice to cry out fervently to keep many souls from entering eternal damnation. Where and when can I meet with you? Or will Satan designed a group of words in your mind that will cause you to conclude that there is no need? Can I show you the destructive days that are upon us? The tragic phenomenal events upon the earth are increasing and will not go away until the righteousness that Elohim ordained for man is fully re-established.

In the Holy Scriptures, the prophets have stated repeatedly that Elohim will judge this world and its inhabitants. Is it possible to find grace in the sight of God? The answer is yes. Even though you may suffer greatly with the evildoers, your soul is preserved in Christ Jesus.

What part of God's judgments will you fulfill? There is not anyone that can escape or be exempted from the standing before the Judgment Seat of Christ. Because you exist and have a soul, you will fulfill these words! You may have concluded that you do not have a soul. Did Satan walk up to you and tell you, with his evil tongue, that you do not have a soul? Well, how did you hear his words? If you did not have a soul, you could not think. If you did not have a soul, you would not be able to read silently. How could you plan to do something if you had to say it aloud or write it down on paper? There would be no reasoning in the world if the people did not have souls. The word *decision* would not exist if you did not have a soul. There would not be dreams and visions in existence if you did not have a soul. There would be no understanding in the world if you did not have a soul. Can flesh and blood store knowledge? It is the soul that remembers, not the dust of the earth after death. If each individual of the human race had only one tongue, chaos and confusion would be everywhere. Furthermore, everyone would have to write down what he or she was going to say to someone else. If you did not have a soul, you would be like a record that lies in silence until someone plays it. The only words that you would hear would be the words proceeding out of your mouth.

When you see a word or thing, do you always open your mouth and utter it? Everything in existence generates a sound. The word *ideology* and many other related words would not be in Webster's Dictionary if man did not have a soul. How could you study without a soul? Would there be a need for a library if you did not have a soul? What classroom in the world would tolerate the noise if every word that people saw was spoken? There would be no thoughts without a hidden tongue.

Call for an assembly of those that cannot hear and speak that they may manifest the Wisdom of God. Ask them if they have souls. Give them things to write with and paper. Also, send for those knowing the art of sign language. They will reveal to you that they can speak, but not to anyone in the natural world. They will also reveal to you that they can naturally hear their words, but not the sounds of anything else. Summon the people that cannot see that they may enlighten you with the Truth. Ask them if they have ever dreamed before. At least one of them, I fully believe, will say yes. The Apostle Paul lost his natural sight for a few days, but saw himself in a vision being restored by God through Ananias.

By now, you should understand that you do have a soul that will be judged for the deeds that you have done in your body.

CHAPTER TWO:
HEAVEN'S RESPONSE TO THE
D. V. CODE

The war to try to destroy the deity of Christ has begun. The vain and corrupted minds of many men and women have fallen prey to the invisible, roaring lion. Satan is now using the press and the media to spread his evil delusions into the minds and hearts of many people. Above all, in the tactical strategies of war, Satan is using a painted picture on a wall. The first question that I want to ask the deceived is why it took you so long to believe a formulated lie! The painting was finished over five hundred years ago.

The hidden purpose of the book and movie is to convince the people that Jesus Christ of Nazareth was only a man like any other man. Can a painted picture on a wall that was made about five hundred years ago, and about 1,400 years after the crucifixion, all of a sudden convey a hidden message of Jesus Christ of Nazareth being married and becoming a biological father? How in the world did you let about four thousand years of prophecies and the fulfillment of all of those prophecies; the people witnessing the Savior of this world who died and was resurrected; who ascended on high and who now is sitting at the right hand of the Father and who was made both Lord and Christ be degraded, by certain demonized men and women, from the Son of God to common manhood? Since a painted picture on a wall has such a great influence upon the minds of people, maybe all of the preachers that are in the world should start painting pictures on walls that would influence the people to stop sinning and killing each other. When the picture was painted, it was an illustration of the past and not a futuristic image. Even though a man is given futuristic knowledge, it is very rare that Elohim shows him the past.

Oh, ye evil and reprobative people of the twenty-first century, how long will you last? Elohim has declared the Truth to this world through his only begotten son, Jesus Christ of Nazareth. When you propagate a lie of this nature among the people, you are personally insulting Elohim, which leads him into a state of great wrath. All of the words in existence that proceeded out of the mouth of God concerning his only begotten son, Jesus Christ, are of the Truth. Ten million painted pictures on walls will never change one jot or one tittle of the written prophecies and their fulfillments. All that you are doing, if you are a believer of this lie, is preparing yourself for eternal damnation in the lake of fire. Can a delusion from the devil destroy the Truth, or is it designed to destroy the minds of men and women? Many of you have become reprobative because you believe this lie!

Is the man that painted the picture wrong for trying to illustrate, in a drawing, one of the greatest events in the history of Eternity? I personally do not think so. It is the twenty-first century demonized hypocritical people who have taken something good and profaned it for monetary gain. Did he really paint the picture to send a cryptic message to be revealed to the twenty-first century inhabitants of this world, or did he fulfill a request for someone he knew whose name was Lodovico Sforza?

If a man had a dear child who painted a picture of him, what would he do or say to that child? Would he rebuke that child, or would he smile and be thankful that his son or daughter was thinking of him? If the child was four years old and painted the picture very unprofessionally, the child would probably get a hug or kiss for trying. The child-minded man Leonardo da Vinci did his best to fulfill the request of Lodovico Sforza. A child of good intent finds grace in the sight of God. Elohim could have stopped him from even drawing the picture to prevent what now is taking place in the minds of evil men and women.

Leonardo, in the painting, portrayed the likeness of whom and what he knew in his time. He did not draw the Cup of Blessing, known as the Holy Grail, because I believe he did not have any idea of how it looked! Only those that were in the upper room know the absolute Truth. Everyone else among man is a part of assumptions, unless God reveals the event unto them. The people in the picture are real portraits, except Jesus Christ, of those who were of his day and time.

Can you lie to yourself after you know the Truth? A lie has no existence! Have we allegorically returned to the Garden of Eden to be deceived again unto the second death, which is the eternal sentencing into the lake of fire? Now you are asking for more of the worst! Everyone is now under the consequence of death, except for a few exceptions and those of the great Rapture. I fully believe that what I am about to say to you is true. Every man and woman that is involved in the promotion and propagation of this satanic lie, whether direct or indirect, is a part of the operations of the Antichrist! Since you have progressed into the consequences of the second death, what are you going to do? You have chosen a lie to become rich. The Lord God Almighty has proclaimed the good news unto this world, and now it is your intention to destroy it. Seven woes are upon you! Satan has sorted out many ways to destroy the name of Jesus Christ of Nazareth without being successful. Well, he will never succeed! Never! The lie is designed to distract the mind from salvation. The words of that deadly lie give men and women the incentive to justify sins and abominations. They will say in their hearts that Jesus Christ of Nazareth was not the Son of God and that everything else concerning him is false. The poison that is in us looks for justification in everything that we do wrong. The book author and the movie producer of this lie will soon drown in their own filth! The prophets spoke well about this generation when one of them said, "Why did the heathen rage, and the people imagine vain things?" Satan wants to relate the notion to the people that the Truth is a lie.

Chapter Three:
Truth Contestation

Today the spirit of Elijah the prophet is upon me. The question about Mother Nature versus the disciplinary actions of God is before me. I will ask you that same question that Elijah asked his people. How long are you going to waver between two opinions? In order to remove all doubt, I need two cities and the inhabitants thereof for the contestation. Since Elijah allowed the prophets of Baal to be first in his day, I only think that it would be right that the city of my choice be used and described first.

Find a city whose entire population is clothed with righteousness. Find a city where purity is in the heart and mind of everyone night and day, continuously. This city must be free of all of those who manifest immoralities mentally and physically. This city's governing body must be holy and totally without deceit. In this city, the dress code must be in accordance with the thoughts of holiness, willingly and at all times. In this city, only the hymns of the Gospel are played on the radio frequencies. The television stations are free of every sound and act that would interfere with the standards of holiness, with no exceptions! The guns, in this city, must be stored, without security, in a certain place where they are to be used for hunting only. This city must not have a police force to enforce the law, because everyone would love his or her neighbor as themselves. Casinos, nightclubs, and liquor stores must be unheard of in this city. The most important element for the city of my choice is that the whole city must be able to worship the Lord our God in the Spirit and in the Truth.

Now it is your turn to make a choice of a city for the contestation. This city and the inhabitants thereof must have experienced many great, phenomenal, and catastrophic events in the past. The inhabitants must all be tested for drug usage. The number of gays and lesbians living in this city must be counted. The number of abortions that have been performed in this city must be declared. We must know how many homicides have happened in this city. We must know how many prostitutes there are in this city. We need to know how many arrests have been made in this city. We need to know if the governmental officials are honest and not corrupt. We need to know how many casinos, nightclubs, and liquor stores are in this city. We need to know if the inhabitants' dress code is honorable or lustful. We must know how many Christians live in this city. We need to know if idol worshipping takes place in this city.

We now have two very different cities for the contestation. Let us give each one an allegorical, fitting name. The first city we will call the Saint's City, and the second one will be called Sin City. The next step in the contestation is to define Mother Nature and the disciplinary actions of God.

The word *nature* is a very evil and deceiving word when it is used to describe the disciplinary acts of God. The truth is that the word is *Natura*, a goddess of Greek mythology. The word is used to remove the causes of catastrophic events, because certain people think that Natura is a mythical, personified woman that controls the forces in the universe. The phrase *Mother Nature* opens the doors to evolutionary thoughts and depicts an escape from reality. When the thoughts of man are made known after a catastrophe, the "how comes" are never considered. The people say it was Mother Nature, and allegorically speaking, that is the end of the sentence.

In the beginning, God created the heaven and the earth. He controls everything that he has made! God made this world to manifest his love. Man has become so evil that he must be chastised back to his God-given senses. From the day that man disobeyed Elohim and sinned, disciplinary measurements have been ordained to keep man from destroying himself. Your response would be this question: How is this God's Love? Let me answer you clearly and plainly. It is far greater to be chastened into eternal life than to be left alone to experience eternal damnation. Your mother and father chastised you for doing something wrong. Was it out of love or hatred? They loved you so much that they would discipline you so that you would become a better person to keep you from ending up in the pits of hell. Most of the people that I know are very appreciative for having been disciplined in their youth. Many of those that were never disciplined ended up in jail, died, or became very bad people. You cannot go beyond the Word of God, which states that he that spares his rod hates his son, but he that loves him chastens him betimes.

Someone said that a recent hurricane could not stop the music. Well, it was not Elohim's intention to stop the music, but to let you know just how easy it would be to remove you from existence because of sins and abominations. If this statement was directed toward Elohim in defiance of what he cannot do, lo and behold—the hurricane seasons have not ended yet. To set the record straight, Elohim can stop the music and those who play it. Only a very evil-minded man would challenge God! You have been spared to say what you have said because of God's great and infinite Grace.

Is there a reason there is death and destruction, or have you perceived that it just happens? Where did death come from? Why does it come upon both man and beast? If it is just something that happens on its own accord, then why will it not just stop on its own accord? The scientists think that in a few years they are going to acquire the knowledge to make someone immortal. How are you going to make someone immortal, when you cannot figure out how to make dust yet? You are a liar and of the father of lies. How can the dust of the earth make immortality? The only way that a man can gain immortality is through Jesus Christ, our Lord. Again, how can you make someone immortal when you cannot begin your own existence? You have already said that there is no God and that you do not have a soul. Where are you going to find the substance to make immortality? Dust and immortality is a very bad combination! Because you do not believe that there is a God, you think that you have a right to do anything that you so desire. Well, you will soon find out that you do have a soul and that your body was made from the dust of the earth.

Elohim wants you to be a part of his household, but you want to bring the devil with you. You want a god that would let you do as you please without any disciplinary actions. Shall I pray for you? Prayer will not eternally help anyone whose name is not in the Lamb's Book of Life. How can I pray for you if you are a future inhabitant of the lake of fire? You want to sin and commit abominable acts of lust. Many of you are striving to find more ways to provoke the wrath of God!

If Elohim will not stop the evil, then who will? If Elohim had allowed Adam and Eve to eat from the Tree of Life, after they sinned there would have been a world of evil in which no one would die! Whether you believe it or not, death was a blessing in disguise. If the days of Noah did not have an end, what kind of world would we be living in today? If there were neither laws nor a lawgiver, who would want to live in this world? Now there is a great lawbreaker on the horizon, and no one wants to stop him, with a few exceptions. Who is going to stop men and women from becoming gays and lesbians? Who is going to stop the unlawful abortions? Who is going to make the schools safe again? Who is going to stop the terrorists in the world? Who is going to stop men from killing each other? Evil is increasing greatly! If Elohim will not stop the Evil, this planet will soon be a very unpleasant place in which to be born.

Come now, all of you, that you may be a witness of the Truth. Many of you have declared to the world that all things evolved out of nothing and that everything that is in existence is a part of nothing. In order that the Truth is made manifest, without any doubt whatsoever, the people in both cities must agree to follow these instructions unwaveringly: All of the inhabitants of Saint's City must be willing to move to Sin City. All of the inhabitants of Sin City must move to Saint's City. Now we have relocated the inhabitants of both cities. The people in both cities are still the same as before. The only thing different is their location. According to scientific data, the inhabitants of a place have no effect on the force they call Mother Nature. Therefore, accordingly, the people that now live in Sin City will begin to suffer greatly because they are now in the path of the force they call Mother Nature. The ungodly inhabitants of Saint's City will think that they are now safe because of the location. Was it the location that spared the people that lived in Egypt in the days of Moses? They were all living in the same place. If death is just something that happens, then why did it happen only to the firstborn of every man and beast of the Egyptians in Egypt? Why did Noah begin to make preparations for the Great Flood 120 years in advance? Did the force you call Mother Nature tell him that she would be making her great appearance? When you have decided to fulfill the words of this contestation, the Lord our God will prove to you that the place where some fictional Mother Nature is active is not what matters, but that these things are influenced by the lives that people live. Destruction comes upon those who commit sins and abominations. When you decide to stop committing sins and abominations, then Elohim will bless you.

Chapter Four:
A Bride's Garment

Oh, how beautiful you are. It has been almost two thousand years. My Father has prepared a great feast for us. In spite of all that you have been through, you still are without spots or wrinkles. The precious atoning blood has made you as white as snow. From the beginning unto this very day, you did not let evil stain your garment. Come now to the judgment seat and be judged. It will be for good. Thousands of swords you have come through. So many kings have tried to keep you from this blessed day, but lo and behold, you are here to be forever. Do you hear the sounds of the earth? The earth is rejoicing. The flowers are growing for the celebration. The beasts of the fields are at peace. The angels of Elohim are with us. Take your places that the Lord God has prepared for you, and let us reign with great joy. Our great enemy has been bound. Oh Abraham, Isaac, and Jacob, we have waited for this day for a long time. All of the Saints which died in hope are here. Look at our bodies that the Lord has made. Now our eyes behold that which we could not see. Our ears are now hearing what we could not hear before. You were in the world, but never became a part of it. Many ungodly and foolish men have said that this day would not come. The deceivers and the deceived have come to their end. Rejoice and be exceedingly glad.

CHAPTER FIVE:
THE MOUTHS OF THE
MEN OF SIN

The Men of Sin are making great preparations for their totalitarian ruler, which is the Man of Sin. The laws of lawlessness are before the ungodly councils of the world to be implemented into law. Sophisticated ways for people to be evil and how to deceive them are their motives. The Devil knows that his appointee, the Man of Sin, will be the dominant physical and false spiritual ruler upon the face of the earth for seven years. Three and a half years of stealthy deception and three and a half years of evil and brutal totalitarianism will be his length of time of fulfillment. He will conquer everyone living during his reign that is false and that is not of God. After the world is deceived, he will then use the deceived to try to destroy the Church and all of those who are of the nation of Israel. Please note that the true Church is in the world, but not of the world. The Man of Sin will come to his deadly end, as will all that is with him when he attempts to destroy the Church and the nation of Israel.

The Men of Sin offer men and women death in disguise for sensual pleasure. You are being conquered by the words that proceed out of the mouths of the Men of Sin. God gave man his senses for righteousness and not for wickedness and evil. The words from their mouths, which are telepathically received from the tongue of the devil, are received into the minds of people, and from the minds, they are accepted into their hearts and are manifested. The devil also gives the deceive, telepathically, the knowledge to cause his words to exist. The difference between the people of God and those who are of the devil is that both of them can hear the same words, telepathically, from the devil or a demon, but those words will only have an effect upon those that accept them into their heart. This only happens when those words become physically manifested through your senses. Let us set forth an example for you, namely a person that commits suicide. This allegorical person is physically perfect with no defects. This person is twenty-four years old, has well-to-do parents, and is well educated. He wants his parents to buy him a car. After his well-to-do parents do not buy him a car, he takes an overdose of sleeping pills and ends his life. After the parents discover what happened, they end their lives by hanging themselves. Was this piece of material, the car, an object of little value that was unobtainable for a short time, the reason three individuals destroyed themselves? Or was it much more? It takes a few seconds, in an accident, for a car to be destroyed. If no one wanted to buy this young man a car, all he had to do was find a job and buy it himself. The whole sum of the senses that God gave to every human being is for survival and worshipping God. At the point of death, every effort is made to sustain life. This young man had a number of reasons to live other than a car. Satan's words of deception persuaded this young man to take his own life. What did the suicidal demons tell him and his parents? Whatsoever the demons related to him had a devastating effect on his eternal existence. It is very apparent that the demons did lie to him, because he thought, after being deceived, that when he destroyed himself, that was the end. The truth is that he ended his earthly life and entered eternal damnation. The same thing that happened to him also happened to his parents.

The words of the Deceiver that are given to the Men of Sin are beginning to be manifested everywhere. My eyes have witnessed the effects of their evil lying words, and my ears have heard the results thereof. The senses of many men and women have accepted their words into their hearts and brought them into existence. What happened in heaven in the beginning? How did the Deceiver recruit one-third of the angelic host to side themselves with him in the rebellion? Was it through silence, or was it by the allegorical expression, "Let's make a deal with great rewards?" Those angels that joined him in the rebellion did not know that their end would be torment without end. The Deceiver was in such a lying mode that he lied to himself. When he said to himself that he would exalt his throne above the stars of God and would be like the Most High, he was lying!

The words of the Deceiver entered the heart of Eve because of what he offered her. She knew the Word of Truth that she had received from Elohim. The sounds of the words from the Deceiver that were sensed by her heart seemed to be more rewarding than the Word of God. However, the truth was that the Word of Elohim meant life and the words of the

Deceiver were unto death. From that day unto this day, the Deceiver has used the same techniques, which are offers unto death.

How are the words and acts of the Deceiver multiplied? The poison of lust, which was accepted by Eve and given to Adam, can only be removed through the Truth. As long as men and women accept the lies of deception, the works of the Deceiver will continue until Jesus Christ destroys him. The Great Flood did not destroy Satan and the demons and their influence upon man. After the cleansing of the Great Flood, man again began to be deceived, for from within the Ark, someone present or an offspring of one of the passengers became a carrier of deception into the world. Now billions of men and women are being deceived.

The Man of Sin, in essence, is the physical mouthpiece of Satan. Satan has been constrained to words and deceiving lying wonders. If the Deceiver had been allowed to use his supernatural power, the world would have been destroyed a long time ago. Fire is used to test gold, and evil is a test of Truth. Perfected faith is not without a test. A lie becomes a lie when the Truth is revealed. Many of you are living by the lies that proceeded out of the mouth of the Devil.

The laws of lies are being practiced all over the world. Men and women have the choice to accept the Word of God or the words of the Deceiver. When all of the lies are exposed through the Truth, then the Kingdom of Heaven will be established. The Saints must go through all of the previously ordained tests that we that are of the Truth may be a part of it forever. All of those that are of the evil lies of the Deceiver will perish with him.

When the Men of Sin speaks, the whole world listens. When all of the pure-hearted saints hear their words, they reject them completely. The Truth will not give evil a place to rest! You are evil because you have accepted the words of evil. Evil is the disobedience of every word that proceeds out of the mouth of God. You have become as garage door openers, the remote controls of which are in the hands of the Men of Sin. Every time they push the buttons, you react to their words. The people in this world are making the mouths of the Men of Sin bigger by feeding them with their silence.

The deceiving plans of the Deceiver are before us and are written in the inspired Word of God so that we can read them. But because men and women are being demonized, which is beyond ignorance, they will fulfill every word that has been written concerning them. There is no manifested wisdom of yourself at all when you are possessed with a demon. There is no wisdom in adultery. There is no wisdom in murder. There is no wisdom in abortion. There is no wisdom in rap music. There is no wisdom in a rapist. There is no wisdom in robbery. There is no wisdom in sodomy. There is no manifested wisdom in anything that is sinful and evil. Sophisticated lying and deceiving techniques are being utilized to destroy the minds of men and women. What mother in her right mind would want to destroy her healthy fetus? What man in his right mind would be intimate with another man? What woman in her right mind would lust after another woman? What man or woman in his or her right mind would show their shame before millions of people for a few temporal dollars? What group of people in their right minds, after witnessing the wonderful works of God, would say that there is no God? What judge in his right mind would justify sodomite binding together laws? The poison of lust is so great that governmental officials, who are not in their right minds, are helping the people with laws so that those people are not able to be in their right minds. The false priest who is secretly a pedophile is not in his right mind when he stands before the congregation in his white robe. The men and women that alter their genders through surgical techniques are definitely not in their right minds. There are whole nations whose minds have been deceived.

God has blessed the soul of man with the unique ability to govern his senses that he may bring forth righteousness in the world. The Men of Sin have decided to try to take away, by removing the ability to reason, the blessings that God put upon man. Is it right for women to come to God's House in minidresses with the kitchen exposed, almost ready to breastfeed a child? Where is the reasoning? When are you going to come to your senses? Did Jesus Christ of Nazareth die on the cross for this kind of behavior? Is this a part of salvation or lust? Is there an intelligent and lawful way to murder children? Is there an intelligent and lawful way to commit suicide? Is there an intelligent and lawful way to rob people? The men and women of the Men of Sin have made all of these acts lawful and a part of illusory intelligence. In the future, the Man of Sin will exalt himself to the thought of being a god, but he will be consumed by the Word of God.

The Men of Sin's treasurer, Master Mammon, is the solicitor who raises funds to finance all of the operations that will cause men and women to inherit the second death. Who paid the billions of dollars for the millions of women to have abortions? The operations of evil are the most costly thing on the face of the earth. When evil is abolished, poverty will cease to exist. No one will ever be wanting for the things necessary for life. We have become slaves for the Men of Sin! The Men of Sin need money for the weapons and for their bluff to instill fear upon the nations in the future. The Men of Sin need money to fund their suicide missions upon innocent people. The Men of Sin need money for the drug epidemic to open the doors of the people's minds for demons! The Men of Sin need money for the pimps and prostitutes to destroy marriages, increase adultery and fornication, and spread venereal diseases. The Men of Sin need lots of money to propagate their lies all over the world. The Men of Sin need money for the False Prophet for his art of deception. Where is all of this money going to come from for the Men of Sin to use for our destruction? All of the funds will come from brainwashed and deceived people! In essence, the national debt of trillions of dollars is the money that the Men of Sin have used for all of their operations of sin and evil.

The Truth is every word that has proceeded out of the mouth of God. The Truth is every word that is proceeding out of mouth of God right at this moment.

The Truth is every word that will proceed out of the mouth of God. All of his words are of the Truth and will not return void. Our health and strength is in righteousness. Our safety is in holiness. Our every need is in worshipping God and keeping his commandments.

Chapter Six:
The Hole in the Wall:
Who am I?

This chapter is for all of those that have the potential of being a part of the inheritance of God. The world loves stardom and people that perform acts of kindness and goodwill toward humanity. The world recognizes fame and riches as a sign of great blessings. Becoming a movie star, winning world-renowned competitions, winning millions of dollars in lotteries, building elaborate mansions, and buying expensive cars, are the ever-growing desires for those who want to be successful in life among men and women. The excitement, the thrill, and the joy over the famous of so many of those that seem to be less fortunate are overwhelming. The autograph signing, the memorabilia, the advertisements, and the idolization of these individuals are manifested all over the world because of things that were done or said by these persons. The theatergoers, the mass media, and advanced communication personnel are constantly waiting to hear and see something new that the rich and the famous might say or do. The world has famed and idolized certain people so greatly that they cannot come out of their homes and into the public in peace. It seems as though all of the things that I have written about are good. Will all of those who are rich and famous inherit eternal life? Many of you will answer and say yes! How can you say yes to this? Jesus Christ of Nazareth, not man, will judge every man and woman for the deeds that were done in their bodies.

It is written: "Follow peace with all men, and holiness, without which no man shall see the Lord." Let us now look through the allegorical hole that is in the wall and see what will be the end of those that seem to be so beautiful and sweet.

You have cosmetically enhanced your face for enticement. You have put on the garments of lust. You have just committed adultery, fictional adultery, fornication, or fictional fornication. Your lips have touched someone who is not your own! The world watches you with great admiration as you take off the garments of lust and clothe yourself in shame. The souls of men long to have you, if they could. The Soaps, that I call the Washing Powder Operas, have destroyed many homes and have made the minds of many men and women filthy. You have entertained millions of minds into sin and death. You have performed the dances of uncleanness. You have broken the pure minds of children. Your good deeds are spoiled by sinning. Your money is made up of sins and abominations, and not pure gold that has been tried in the fire. Your works are the deeds of darkness. You are sitting in the seat of delusions. When was the last time that you attended church services? When was the last time that you prayed a sincere prayer? Oh, woman and man, don't you realize that the judgments of God are at hand? Wake up and live! Change your ways and repent! After all of these acts of unrighteousness, you appear before the world to be rewarded and to display the pretence of innocence. If this was the end of it, I would not have written this chapter.

Satan has blinded you with the thoughts of his mind. He is using you for his deadly cause. Money is a temporal commodity that becomes useless in the hour of death. Without the garment of righteousness, you will appear before God naked! Will your fame and riches change the outcome of the judgment after death? Will you be able to bribe God with your beauty and riches? Are you famous in heaven? What is Jesus Christ saying about you to his Father? Satan and all of the demons think that you are doing a great job, because without a change you will inherit their same fate in the future. Do you have the ability to remove the scales from your eyes so that you can see? Today, I am your eye doctor; God has blessed me to remove the scales from your eyes. After you have read this chapter, you will begin to see. This is the only thing that I can do for you. There is only one star of essence among mankind, which is the Star of Jacob, who is Jesus Christ of Nazareth. Your stardom is less than a spark before God, and it shall soon vanish away and be no more! God's grace and the life that you live determine your future. You have to decide in your mind if you want to continue in sin or become a part of God's great saving grace.

CHAPTER SEVEN: THE CYCLE OF DEATH

The word *death* and the subject of it are not readily and easily comprehended through the intuitional mind of man. Elohim, who created all things, can give the understanding and the mysteries concerning death to whomsoever he will. We have heard words in our ears telling us that once you are dead, you are done. These are not the words of the Truth! If we were finished with life at the time of death, the fear of dying would only be for nothing. If we were finished with life when we died, the ordinances of sin and abominations would only be for societal well-being. The world is trying to define life as if it were a leaf on a tree. If there were no consequences after death, then you could do anything that you wanted to do as long as no mental or physical harm would come to anyone else.

For a better understanding of death, we need to start from the beginning. God told Adam that the day that he ate of the Tree of Knowledge of Good and Evil, he would surely die. Was this, in essence, the tree of death? Or was it because of what Adam and Eve became? The glory of God can forever sustain whosoever he will. God blessed Adam and Eve from an eternal life of sin and evil when he drove them out of the Garden of Eden. God is Life. Did Adam really have to eat of the Tree of Life to live forever? Or did he only have to just obey God? Elohim has the power to do whatsoever he will! To the best of my knowledge, I believe that this was a great test. The test was for Adam and Eve and for the entire human race. If it was not a test, God would not have created the tree and allowed it to grow in the first place. Jesus Christ of Nazareth is the only man that has ever passed all of his tests!

Life begins with God and is not just a happenstance phenomenon. Everything that you see that is moving had its beginning with Elohim. The existence of man consists of a soul, a spirit, and a body. When these three are united together, you become a person, which is a living soul. Death is the separation of the soul and spirit from the body. Is there a difference between *died* and *was killed*? Yes, there is a great difference!

From this point in this chapter, the word *separation* will be used to represent the word *death* for more understanding and clarity. Did Abel die according to the Word of God, or did Cain kill him and then he died? Cain destroyed the body and caused an unauthorized separation. The soul and spirit of Abel still exists. Why did not God stop him from killing his brother and causing that separation? God allows man to manifest the things that are in his heart that he might judge them and that they may witness for themselves whether they are perpetually good or perpetually evil. Murder is an unauthorized separation of the soul and spirit from the body. Elohim is the only one that has the authority to ordain a separation! He has the authorization, because he is the owner of the life, to choose any form or manner in existence that he so desires to cause separation. The separations are for judgments and cleansing.

In many cases, a righteous man or woman leaves this world as a kiss from God, and many of the evildoers' departures are caused by the earned separation of destruction. Enoch's departure occurred without a separation. He walked with Elohim into eternal life. His judgment was made manifest by being translated. Jesus Christ of Nazareth sealed the new covenant with his own blood, which cleansed the soul of sin and evil. He brought back the Tree of Life for every accepted human being that has been or will be cleansed. The apostles, and many of the martyrs, are witnesses of the new covenant with a blood baptism. A person of the Truth will give his or her life to be a witness for the Truth.

Why did God destroy Sodom and Gomorrah? He would have spared the city of Sodom if there were ten righteous individuals that lived there. Were there women and children in the city that were counted worthy of being righteous? The truth is that perpetual evil must be cleansed from the earth for earthly habitation from time to time. If Elohim would allow evil to multiply without consequences, then evil would dominate the world! Perpetual evil is the growth and continuation of sin and abomination in a group, nation, or city that will be carried from generation to generation by the offspring of the group. This is the reason Elohim destroyed those cities.

What is going to happen to this world in the very near future? The nations are stockpiling weapons of mass destruction. The nations are in competition to find out who can make the greatest weapon that can kill the most people. A piece of land has become a god. Killing is for lies! The people of certain religions have no respect for life, not even for themselves or their own dearly beloved children. The great cleansing in which all of those that offend will take place in the near future. The greatest weapon of Satan is the ability to use words to cause people to destroy themselves. His next greatest weapon is the cunningness to deceive people into being a part of God's great wrath. It is Satan's desire for men and women to be separated to enter the realm of eternal damnation.

If you died and passed out of existence, there would be no need for a judgment, and the only consequences of sin and abomination would be the suffering you suffered while living, which you thought would completely end after you died. Once you are brought into existence, your soul and spirit will continue to exist forever. Man can cause a separation but cannot destroy the soul and spirit out of existence. The separation that Elohim ordained because of evil is a departure which is not of flesh and blood. The flesh and blood, which came from the earth, returns to it after the separation. All of us came from Adam, which is the name of the earth. The soul and spirit now come before the Judgment Seat of Christ after the separation.

Before we continue into the mysteries of separation, I want you to know that Adam and Eve are the only ones that have a beginning age. Everyone else only knows how long he or she has been in the world. You do not know the age of your soul and spirit.

A selfish early separation is not of God, but is of man. For example, the surgeon general has stated that smoking is hazardous to your health. Nevertheless, because of the poison of lust (and our last name is still Adam, who is our greatest grandfather, according to the flesh), man is still making billions of cancer sticks for early separations! Do you really want to live the number of days that Elohim has allotted to you? I don't think so. If the people in the world wanted you to live, all they would have to do is stop making the cancer sticks. The international economy is being funded by causing unauthorized separations. Assistant suicidal acts are unauthorized separations! Where is the mercy among mankind? Have men and women changed the meaning of love to capital gain? Do people really love the gift of life anymore? Is there a new law on the books that says, "Love thy neighbor for capital gain?" Is the new word for genocidal murder *abortion*?

Oh Lord God, in the name of your only begotten son, Jesus Christ of Nazareth, please help us. The whole world has peaked as it was in the days of Noah. The evil has penetrated even into the nations that have feared you in the past. Please come and save us from ourselves and deliver us unto thy righteousness that we may live. The hope for peace is gone. The weapons for war have increased greatly. The minds of men and women are being demonized. The saints are becoming weak. Your laws for life and freedom have been rejected. Please come and help us. Please don't let us be the ones that brought holiness to a shame! It is better to die in hope than to live in shame. If I am now ready to be accepted into thy kingdom, do not let me live to be rejected.

Chapter Eight:
To the House of David

Beloved of the beloved, where are you? I have words of hope for you. Do not turn your ears from the words of my mouth. I am the least among the brethren. The Spirit of Adoption has adopted me into the priesthood. The Lord Our God has anointed me to write this chapter unto you.

Oh, house of Jacob, the nations are against you, and the judgments are at hand. The people have strayed away from the ways of Elohim and the protection that he has ordained for you have been withdrawn. The armies of the world will come up against you to inhabit the blessed city. You have a great need to listen to me. You know that you cannot change one jot or one tittle of true prophecy.

First of all, I must convince you that the Spirit of Truth is upon me and that it is true that Elohim has given me the words to say to you. If the words that I am about to say to you are true and will come to pass, then you must consider that everything else is confirmed and established. If the words that I am about to say to you are false, then you are at liberty to call me a liar and in league with the devil.

To the elect of God in the House of David, the time has come for the blindness in part to be removed from your eyes. Hope begins with the Truth, and faith is the beginning of hope.

It is written: "in that day, there shall be a fountain opened to the House of David and to the inhabitants of Jerusalem for sin and for uncleanness." It is also written: "for I would not, brethren, that ye should be ignorant of this mystery, lest ye should be wise in your own conceits; that blindness in part is happened to Israel, until the fullness of the Gentiles be come in." And so all Israel shall be saved. As it is written: "There shall come out of Zion the Deliverer, and shall turn away ungodliness from Jacob: For this is my covenant unto them, when I shall take away their sins."

Wake up, oh Jacob. Awaken from your sleep of unbelief. The Lord Our God has sanctified his word in my heart to give to you. It has been about two thousand years since your forefathers were judged for crucifying the anointed one that brought the destruction upon Jerusalem. If you are looking for a different one, Eternity only has one to give. No one else was worthy, and never will be among men, who could be an acceptable atonement for our sins. If I am not telling you the truth, then find me a man that is without spot or blemish, with no guile found in his mouth, who can raise the dead, give sight to the blind, cause the dumb to talk and the deaf to hear, heal all manner of diseases, and cast out devils. Find him who bruised the head of Satan and removed the sting of death, who descended to set the captive free, who rose from the dead and was glorified to sit at the right hand of the Almighty God in glory. Please find me the man that did all of these things, and I will rejoice in hope. But I am rejoicing greatly, because Jesus Christ of Nazareth has fulfilled every written word of the scriptures that the prophets of old foreknew concerning him.

Ever since Moses declared that the Lord thy God would raise up unto you a prophet from the midst of you and your brethren and that like unto me, unto him ye shall hearken, you have been waiting for the fulfillment of his words. Love, not war, conquers the souls of men. Elohim has the divine plans for eternal redemption. Your thoughts of a military conqueror are vain and without hope. The whole human race needed a redeemer to redeem them from the works of the devil. Your enemies needed someone to change their ways. If conquering was the solution, then you would be warring until the end of time. Satan would always raise up a nation to hate you. When the Lord Our God manifested his great love to all nations through his only begotten son, Jesus Christ of Nazareth, there was hope. When the Messiah returns, which is the Word of God; who is even the same Jesus whom ye crucified and whom Elohim has made both Lord and Christ, he will rule all nations with a rod of iron. Jerusalem will then be at peace.

The test of Truth that I now set before you is the removal of the scales that are over your eyes. When the scales of time are removed from your eyes, you will begin to see the Truth. When this takes place, you must be a witness to the brethren that they may be a part of the same.

The Fountain of Life, which was ordained and opened about two thousand years ago, is now opened unto you. If your forefathers would have accepted the Truth and the life, the scriptures would not have been fulfilled. The omniscient Elohim knows that the day will come when the House of David will be given the understanding to fulfill the scriptures.

Belief is the door of the Fountain of Life. You must believe that Elohim sent his only begotten son into the world to save his people from their sins. You must believe that the Redeemer was born into the world by a virgin. You must believe that Elohim has said, "This is my beloved son, in whom I am well pleased." You must believe that he was crucified and was in the heart of the earth for three day and three nights. You must believe that God raised him up from the dead to be both Lord and Christ.

The preparation is repentance, which is the rejection of all ungodliness and the retention of unfeigned holiness. The outward public confession of baptism in the name of Jesus Christ of Nazareth for the remission of sin is the final step of all that you can do. After this, the Holy Spirit will then give you the everlasting water of life from the precious atoning blood of Jesus Christ, our Lord. Amen.

I have words of understanding for you if you would only believe. The Antichrist is going to deceive you. To be completely aware of his evil course, you must become a part of the New Covenant. The New Testament is a confirmation of the passing away of the Old Covenant. Hidden, unknown suffering is greater than it would be if you knew what was going to come upon you. Do not let the salvation of millions of your people be lost through unbelief and ignorance.

I will be asking Elohim to speak to one of the leaders of the House of David in a dream or vision that the leader can be a confirmed witness that what I am saying is the truth.

Chapter Nine: The Sounds of the Truth

The words from the mouth of the Son of Perdition are being set forth for his totalitarian kingdom. The inhabitants of the world, except the saints, have accepted his words of desecration, which are unto death and destruction. You are being deceived out of your eternal, blessed inheritance. Satan and the fallen angels have received their judgment already. Their proper and earned inheritance is the lake of fire and torment without an end. The words of the Truth are being profaned to keep men and women out of the Kingdom of God. There is nothing in existence that can destroy the Truth, which came forth out of the mouth of Elohim! The sounds of the Truth are being removed or changed to allow people to become wicked and evil without the knowledge of any known consequences. In this very important chapter, if it is God's will, we will set forth the hidden words of the Second Death unto you.

Before we begin to make known the hidden understanding of the Second Death, Satan has already said to you or someone that there is no such thing in existence. Where did those words come from, since you did not open your mouth to speak them? There is a reason you heard them. The words that you heard were spoken for the rejection of the very thing that we want you to understand, namely the Second Death. What is the thing that is in you that can generate sounds of words? You need to find out how and when it became a part of you. On the other hand, you need to find out how you became a part of it. The truth is that the dust of earth is still the dust of the earth. Your body was formed to be separated from the soul for judgment. Your body was united together with your soul for earthly life and deed manifestation. A part of you is from the mouth of God, which will never die. When Elohim shared the breath of life with the man that he formed from the dust of the earth, the breath that went into him made him an eternal creature. God did not breathe into the nostrils of any other creature. When Elohim breathed into the nostrils of Adam, we became God's sons and daughters. When Elohim breathed upon us the second time, we became royalty.

It is written: "the soul that sinneth, it shall die." The word die, in this verse of the Holy Scriptures, is not the death as of an animal. The animal that dies or is killed is completely finished with life when it happens. All of those that are a part of evil, including the evolutionists and the secularists, are trying their very best to make you believe that you are just an intelligent animal that has the same fate as the other animals. If the forces of evil can convince men and women that they are only high-class mammals, then humanity will have no desire whatsoever to be righteous and holy. Satan wants the world to become so evil that Elohim will destroy it. But this will never happen, because the savior of this world, who is Jesus Christ of Nazareth, has atoned with his precious blood for the everlasting and eternal existence which belongs to all of those that are upright and pure. If you want to be like an animal, Satan has the knowledge to help you be like one and worse! If you want to be saved, Elohim, through Jesus Christ, will greatly help you gain his salvation for an everlasting life!

No man or woman in existence should have the desire to be a part of the Second Death. If you fully understood the depths of the knowledge of the

Second Death, you would repent immediately! To understand the Second Death, you need to know something about pain. Does the dust of the earth feel pain? If pain did not exist, then the Second Death would only be a perception and not absolute. If there were no pain, there would be no need for judgments. If there were no pain and suffering in existence, then who would need salvation? If pain and suffering did not exist, *protection* would be an insignificant word. Without pain, there would be no warning of injury or death. Pain is one of the greatest parts of the sense of touch. God ordained pain for protection and disciplinary control. When anyone is in his or her right mind, he or she will do almost anything to keep from experiencing pain and suffering. Will pain and suffering go away after you die? If pain and suffering were connected with the dust of the earth, then you would be free of it after death. However, pain and suffering are not a part of the dust of the earth. Pain and suffering will be a part of the soul and spirit of man until it is removed by Elohim. I speak on the behalf of all of those whose names are in the Lamb's Book of Life. Pain and suffering will increase, which is the Second Death for all of those whose names are not in the Lamb's Book of Life.

It is written: "Blessed and holy is he that hath part in the first resurrection: on such the Second Death hath no power, but they shall be priests of God and of Christ, and shall reign with him a thousand years." Many of you have made the choice of living in a way that will send you to the Second Death after you are deceased from this earthly life. There is a choice of eternal happiness that many of you have rejected because of pride. Since you have lifted up yourselves with the poison of pride, you will see whether the Second Death is real or not. When you find out the Truth, no one will be able to help you. You will know the truth forever and forevermore. To reveal the Truth to you before you experience what I have been trying to keep you from, in a few days Elohim will cause the sun to let you feel a taste of the Second Death. Whether you will have the opportunity to repent or not, I do not know.

Chapter Ten: Truth Court III

You may have wondered why I keep writing to you about the Truth Court. Well, it is about the love for humanity to keep you from destroying yourselves. In the courts all over the world, the Truth is supposed to be disclosed and made known in every case. When the Truth is disclosed, the innocent are vindicated and the evil ones are punished. But if the courts are corrupt and evil themselves, then true justice will not be manifested. Because of the corruption, the courts are only a form of justice to pacify the people.

The *Roe versus Wade* case should have never entered the mind of a sane and intelligent human being. How can insanity judge insanity? Do you really know whom you are killing without a cause? Did you have a beginning? Who gave you a chance to be what you are? Was it justice for your mother to let you live? So if it was justice for your mother to let you live, then why is it justice to destroy the beginnings of life? This is an example of formulated justice, which is, in reality, insanity!

The Truth Court is allegorical, and it has prevention and preservation in mind. Even though the cases are real, the outcomes can be prevented. The Truth Court is a place of words for a pretrial to get you to come to your senses before you are judged in the future before the Judgment Seat of Christ. The Truth Court is also a place of grace where the verdict is used to prick the heart for repentance. Our Lord and Savior Jesus Christ said that you shall know the truth, and the truth shall make you free. It is in my heart to make known the Truth to the world. Jesus Christ of Nazareth, who is the son of the living God, has given the Truth to this world. He has offered the human race life by dying for it on the cross.

Many good people in the world are only being deceived. If the cases that are brought before the world in the Truth Court can disclose the art of deception, millions of people can be saved from the wrath of Elohim. The Evil High Council of Darkness consists of a few embodied individuals in high places. Those that are a part of this totalitarian establishment use innocent people for their works of darkness. This chapter is included so that the innocent may have an opportunity to escape the White Throne Judgment. If you are one of those who will be summoned to the White Throne Judgment, this chapter is not for you.

Case Name: The Spirit of Mercilessness

Plaintiff: Life and the Voices of the Truth

Defendant: Doctor Eor, Mr. and Mrs. Edaw, and the daughter of Mr. and Mrs. Edaw

Life and the Voices of the Truth: We want to know from you, why did you destroy the beginning of that child? You went to college to become a doctor to help people. You learned how to use medical techniques and medicine to promote life and healing. At no time in any of your courses in college did you learn how to hurt people. All that you learned was for the well-being of humanity. Did you promote life when you performed the abortion? If there was no life in the fetus, then why did you have to destroy it? Look at yourself and think! Is this an intelligent act or an act of sophisticated insanity? Is this how you practice medicine? Did you heal the mother or make her the prime accomplice? Is all of that education that you received from college for this? Are you so greedy for gain that you would destroy life? What did you gain? Well, let me tell you what you have gained besides a few hundred dollars. You gain the loss of your dignity and honor. A dedicated doctor who fears God would never do any such thing. Are you one of the new Pharaohs? Is this an ordained depopulation tactic?

Doctor Eor: The Supreme Court has given us the right to perform these procedures. We are very intelligent doctors with the care of the patient in mind. We have studied the laws of life, and it is certain that life only begins after birth. We have not done anything wrong or evil. Even though the sight of the procedure is not pleasant to the eyes, it is only an aggregate of cells together with their intercellular substance that form a fetus. The mother and the father made the decision for me to perform this procedure. If this is wrong, then they are the ones that will be held accountable. It is my job to satisfy the patient to the best of my ability.

Life and the Voices of the Truth: Is the Supreme Court your god? Did the Supreme Court give you life? Is there life in blood? Do nerves have feelings? At what time does life experience pain? Do you know what happened while you were in your mother's womb? Since you have proclaimed the knowledge of the mysteries of life, can you tell me when your soul became a part of you? Elohim ordained life and care for the soul that he has ordained for a certain body. Elohim, through whomsoever he will, causes the soul, spirit, and body to be united together for deed manifestation. Elohim has ordained the earth for deed manifestation. Satan has given you his mind and his thoughts to interfere with Elohim's divine order. Elohim is the only one that has the authority to open and close the matrix! He can make a woman barren, or he can bless her by allowing her to have many children. You do not have the right or the authority to make decisions for Elohim. It is impossible for you and all of the forces in existence to stop or destroy Elohim's divine order of deed manifestation! Satan's hidden purpose is to make sure that the innocent blood of conception is on your hands. Without repentance, you will be a part of that great White Throne Judgment. May God have mercy on your merciless soul.

Mr. Edaw, where is the wisdom that God instilled within you? God gave you more reasoning than he gave to your wife. Did your wife persuade you to agree with her and the evil one that convinced her to have your unborn son or daughter destroyed? If this is so, then your wife is a deceived mediator between you and the devil. Your wife was healthy and experienced no complications whatsoever. You have a well-paying job. God has already blessed you to accommodate the new arrival. For what reason under heaven did you have to agree with your wife? God has already blessed you with your own life. Your mother, whom I honor greatly, never had the thought of destroying you or letting someone else interfere with the beginnings of your existence. We are ashamed of you! Don't you know better? We are displeased with you because you were appointed the head of your household. Has Satan become your head? Lo and behold, the innocent blood of conception is on your hands.

Mr. Edaw: I admit my guilt to this court. I love children. My mother loved me so much. My wife is very persuasive. I agreed with her to please her. Now I understand that without a beginning, no child would exist. I also understand that if my mother had done the same thing to me before I was born, I would not be here today. Sir, I thank you for being kind enough to open the doors of the Truth Court to help me come to my senses.

Life and the Voices of the Truth: Mrs. Edaw, why did you want to have an abortion? Is there anything wrong with the will of God? There is a period of suffering in childbearing, but it turns into joy after the child is born into this world. The ordained order of childbearing was given to married women to replenish the earth, which is a great part of your salvation. The suffering creates a great bond between the mother and the child. We know of a great woman and mother that birthed twenty-two children into this world. Fourteen of them helped to replenish the earth. From the offspring of the fourteen, she now has about three hundred grandchildren, great-grandchildren, and great-great grandchildren. This great woman is alive and well. The blessings of the Lord our God are upon her. You have birthed one into this world and have prevented one from coming into this world by an evil act. In the days of old, women would beg God to open up their wombs that they might not be barren and suffer reproach among the people. Now people are trying to an extreme degree to not bring forth a child into the world. You have exalted yourself beyond the will of God. Woman, you are guilty! Do you know what mercy is? Your mother showed you great mercy. That child is a part of you!

Mrs. Edaw: This is my body, and I have a right to make my own decision about whether I should birth a child into this world. The mothers are the ones that suffer and sometimes die when they give birth to a child. The Supreme Court has ruled on having an abortion, and it is legal to have the procedure done. The men are not the ones that suffer. That is the reason it is so easy for them to be against it. Let them start having children and then let them see what they would say.

Life and the Voices of the Truth: Mrs. Edaw, we want you to know that your mother suffered for you when you were born into this world. Your grandmother suffered when your mother was born. Your great-grandmother suffered for your grandmother when she came into this world. The truth is that every woman that has birthed a child into this world has suffered. Many have died in childbearing. How much do you love your daughter? A dear mother would give her life for the life of her child. The bowels of mercy that were established in woman caused a great bond to be formed between her and the child that she births into the world. The suffering creates that bond. Mrs. Edaw, you are trying to convince this court that you did not have your unborn child destroyed. Where did the life in you come from? Do you own your life, or was it given to you? After you suffered to bring your daughter into this world, the life that was given to you was not taken away. Life is a great gift from God. Do you think that your body is yours? If you think so, then you are terribly wrong. It belongs to Elohim, who is the great creator.

Mrs. Edaw: Millions of women have had abortions before. Why am I the one that is being prosecuted?

Life and Voices of the Truth: We chose you because we wanted you to be the person that repented and confessed so that other women would stop destroying the unborn children. Your daughter is being intimate with her boyfriend. She did not tell you yet, but she is three months pregnant. She is going to do the same thing that you did to your unborn child. What are you going to say to her? You are an evil example for her. She is going to say that because you had an abortion, she can have one as well. The undisclosed tragic thing that we want to tell you is that she is going to die if she has the procedure! If you really love your daughter, you are going to repent and help her.

Mrs. Edaw: You are trying to blackmail me!

Life: Mrs. Edaw, this is not about blackmailing you, but it is about salvation for you, your daughter, and every other woman that believes in having abortions and will listen to you. You have a great decision to make. If you will not show mercy for your daughter, whom you have birthed into the world, then we will rest our case. But if you decide to allow what God has given every mother—the bowels of mercy—to be brought forth, then you shall live to repent and be blessed. Your mission is to confess to the God of Life and your daughter that you were wrong for having an abortion. She will listen to you because she loves you. You must tell her to get married as soon as possible. You must tell her to be an honorable and respectable mother to her child.

Mrs. Edaw: Who are you? Please show me the path that I must follow to save my daughter and her unborn child. I was wrong! All of the women that had abortions were wrong! Forgive me, oh Lord God Almighty. Please spare the life of my daughter. I make my confession with tears. Please hear me!

Life: The mysteries of life are past finding out. God will not give this adulterous generation this understanding. In the future, you will understand. Thank God for giving you and your daughter an opportunity to repent. Without repentance, you and your daughter would end up in the lake of fire.

This case had a good ending. The jury was dismissed because she repented. The Spirit of Mercilessness departed from her mind because of love. If all of the mothers would let the love of God rule them, the innocent blood of the unborn would not cry out to God.

Chapter Eleven:
The Difference Between a Demon and a Microdemon Infestation

The words *demon possessed* have always been used to characterize a person of violent and uncivilized behavior. Possession has also been classified as being supernatural and as the embodiment of an evil spirit. The world has used replacement words for *demon possessed*. This chapter is included for the exposure of those who are possessed with microdemons.

There are billions of people that are unaware that they have been infested with microdemons. The nickname for this infestation of microdemons that I will be using is Little Legion. The *Legion in the Word of God* will be used for the manifested demons. Some might think that there is no difference between the two. Through the will of Elohim, Jesus Christ, and the Holy Spirit, I pray that I will be able to enlighten the readers in this chapter.

The word demon is another name for a fallen angel. In essence, a demon is a thrown-out angel that is without a possible chance of being accepted back into heaven and being holy. Satan is not classified as a demon, but he is their leader. The knowledge of how many of these fallen angels were cast out with him is unknown to man. The sum of them is given as being a third part of the angelic host during the rebellion. Since there is no hope, whatsoever for Satan and his angels, their works are ones of hopelessness and revenge.

A residential demon does not come into a body to leave. The demon comes to be a part of that individual until death. Only through the power of God in the name of Jesus Christ of Nazareth can a demon be cast out. After being cast out, or after the death of the person or animal, the demon will seek for another dwelling place in which to live. God created everything in existence. Everything that God made was good. Elohim did not corrupt his creation. The archangel Satan and some of the angels corrupted

God's creation. Ever since Satan and his deceived angels rebelled against God, the omnipotent Elohim has been working on cleansing and manifestation. It was not that Elohim lacked the knowledge of what was going to take place, but that his divine will was brought into existence. In summation, Elohim can do whatsoever he pleases. Blessed be his holy name! There is no one in existence that can tell him what he must do.

From the understanding that I have received, I believe that we are here for deed manifestation to replace the angels that rebelled against God. The bottom line is this: If Satan and his angels can cause you to rebel against God on earth through disobedience, then you are a part of his manifested host. I certify to the highest degree that there will never be another rebellion in heaven. Elohim will thoroughly cleanse his creation through his son Jesus Christ of Nazareth. Satan and his angels know that their time is short. They are saving the worst for the last.

First, you must understand that Satan and his destroying demons do not have reproductive organs. Their evil motive is mass recruitment, which means that they recruit everyone that they possibly can. Satan even attempted to recruit Jesus Christ of Nazareth into his realm of hopelessness. Since Satan and his evil host do not have the power to be omnipresent, they come and conquer the minds of people. They influence the mind to accept their evil works of darkness! They establish their hold on the mind with their words of perdition. When they do leave, that person becomes infested with their motives, their desires, their ways, their words, and everything else that is rebellious. After this takes place, the only one that can set you free is Elohim, through his only begotten son, Jesus Christ of Nazareth.

A free Saint of God cannot be contaminated with this Little Legion. The precious atoning blood of the Passover Lamb that is within us will keep the destroyers out. A free Saint is freed to become as one of the angels in Heaven. Everyone whose name is written in the Lamb's Book of Life will become as the angels in Heaven. The Word of Truth protects the saved minds of the people of God. The comforter, which is the Holy Ghost, teaches and guides everyone that has been ordained to receive the gift of eternal life. I pray to God Almighty that I am one of them!

It would be very offensive to describe the permanent dwelling places of many fallen angels. The signs of the inward dwelling of a fallen angel are the permanent loss of one or more of your senses and the inability to control certain bodily functions. When Jesus Christ returns and the healing by his hand is made manifest, then the people of hope will understand.

When Elohim breathed into the nostrils of Adam, he gave him much more than the ability to move and function. To the best of my knowledge, Elohim did not breathe into the nostrils of a woman, but he put Adam to sleep and took a part of him to make him a wife. Elohim gave Adam the wisdom to perform his will and to be holy. Elohim gave Eve the wisdom and the ability to learn from her husband, Adam. The desire for more knowledge than what was in God's divine will was the beginning of our downfall. The wisdom that Elohim gave to Adam can be seen today in man's ability to give names to and to identify with words, according to God's will, everything that is in the earth. The evil works of darkness are summed up in one word, which is rebellion.

To intensify the rebellion against Elohim, it is Satan's desire to turn the whole creation into chaos. To certify the fact that this is true, Satan and the fallen angels corrupted the people so greatly that only eight individuals in the days of Noah escaped the destruction of the Great Flood. This is the purpose of the microdemon infestation, which is being manifested all over the world.

Where did the knowledge of being naked come from? Even though Elohim is omniscient, he did not relate the knowledge of nakedness to Adam when he breathed into his nostrils. So where did the knowledge of nakedness come from? Did the serpent tell them that they were naked? Was it the fruit that Elohim made, or was it that the fruit that he made was infested, by Satan, with the poison of lust, which caused him to understand that he was naked? The commandment that was given to both of them to obey was not to eat from that specified tree. The serpent must have been the first creature to eat the infested fruit of lust, because he became the mouth piece for the communication between Eve and Satan. I must say this loudly and clearly: The vessels for the mouthpiece of Satan, since the beginning, have multiplied so greatly that the people who are falling away from God are being seduced into the works of darkness.

Where did all of the knowledge of being so evil come from? Can fruit talk? If the fruit talked and gave Adam and Eve the knowledge to be evil, then someone needs to find that fruit and destroy it. However, common sense will let you know that it was not the fruit, but what was put into the fruit. The drugs that are being deployed around the world do not talk, but they become a gateway for demonic activity. Becoming high, as it is called, destroys the inability to think. The demons lie in wait to deceive and destroy when this happens. Have you ever heard of someone getting high and doing something good? Drugs have always caused the mind to generate evil.

The serpent was the mouthpiece for the devil, and the fruit became the agent of the poison of lust. The poison of lust is the knowledge from the mouth of Satan of everything that God hates. The spirit of lust is the exact opposite of the works of the Holy Ghost. The Holy Ghost, which is the sent comforter, leads and guides the saints of God in all of the ways of truth. The Spirit of Lust leads and guides the deceived into all of the ways of death and damnable destruction. The knowledge of evil consists of the words of rebellion. Before the fall, Adam and Eve did not have the knowledge to become evil. After the poison was eaten, they possessed the doorway, which is telepathic, for all of the ways and desires of the devil. The poison was not just for the curse of death, but for the destruction of the soul also. Even though they became unclean, Elohim did not destroy them. He punished Adam and Eve by expelling them from being the blessed inhabitants of the Garden of Eden. The Tree of Life was also in the Garden of Eden. It was a great act of Elohim's grace that Adam and Eve did not have an opportunity to eat from the Tree of Life after they disobeyed God. If anyone, by chance, had found the Garden of Eden before Jesus Christ died, they would have never lived to show or tell someone else. The Cherubim and the flaming sword were not put there to just frighten someone away.

Where did the knowledge to perform abortions come from? It is very apparent that it came from an evil source. Those that perform the procedures and have it done are accepted as intelligent and law-abiding citizens. These individuals do not readily seem to be demon possessed. But while the evil procedure is being done, the demons are at work. With no mercy for life, with no fear of God, blind to hope, and with no regard for righteousness, the pseudointelligent medical doctor, the pseudohonorable doctor, the highly paid doctor that went to college to obtain a doctoral degree in philosophy, picks up a sterilized knife and murders an innocent unborn child without a cause. When the abomination is completed, he washes his hands and is accepted among his peers and the world. I want the world to know that these men and women are greatly infested with microdemons.

The highly honored priests that clothe themselves with the garments of holiness, stand before the congregation as being pure and holy and administer the Eucharist, pull off their clothes and perform the abominable act of sodomy with someone's innocent and chaste child, and rape a sister of the faith that becomes pregnant or is forced to have an abortion are infested with microdemons. The works of devils sometime use the form of godliness for their evil disguise.

God made Adam, who was a man. He looked like a man and acted like a man. Elohim gave Adam the will to be intimate with Eve, his wife. God made Eve, who was a woman. She looked like a woman and acted like a woman. Elohim gave Eve the will to be intimate with Adam, her husband. The words that you are about to read are the results of what has happened to many men and women. When Satan and his angels were thrown out of heaven, they were rejected forever. When men and women are rejected forever, it is called reprobation. Reprobation from Elohim is a sign of a person who is without hope and mercy. The abominable acts of reprobation can be clearly seen in this lost and untoward generation. If you became a bisexual, a homosexual, a lesbian, or any other kind of evil, inordinate, intimate individual through demonic influences, there may be a ray of hope for you. However, if Elohim turned you over to a reprobate mind to do these wicked and inconvenient things, then there is no hope for you whatsoever. In the essence of truth concerning this rejection, God allows whosoever definitely wants to do these evil things the liberty to do them. The consequence of reprobation is the Second Death.

Every soul that Elohim made has telepathic abilities. It may seem that we do not have this supernatural ability, but we do. If you did not have this ability, then Elohim would have to write everything that he wanted to say to you. If you did not have this unique ability, the Holy Spirit could not lead and guide you in all of the ways of the Truth. If the angels did not have the ability to be telepathic, then how could they help us? They would be limited to only a physical force. Dreams and visions are given to a person telepathically from Elohim. Inventors receive knowledge from Elohim, telepathically, for good. Every true minister of God is under the guidance of the Holy Spirit through telepathy. There are innumerable prayers that are prayed telepathically.

Evil and wicked thoughts consist of evil words. Pure and good thoughts consist of righteous words. The mind is a place where thoughts come together to converse. The words that come from the soul are your thoughts. Deceptive thoughts are kept within and not revealed from the mouth. The telepathic words that come from the outside and enter the mind can be Elohim; Jesus Christ; the Holy Spirit; an angel; Satan; or a fallen angel, which is a demon. The content of the words that you hear identifies who it is. There may be a few men and women in existence that have the ability to communicate with each other telepathically. Intermediate telepathy is the norm between two individuals. Elohim can reveal the thoughts of someone to another. I believe that telepathy is the sixth sense. This sixth sense is the doorway that demons use to control and destroy the minds of men and women. Before Adam and Eve disobeyed Elohim, Satan could not speak to them telepathically. He had to use someone, and that was the serpent. After the fall, Satan gained access to our minds. This is the reason Elohim gave them the commandment of not eating the fruit from the Tree of Knowledge of Good and Evil. Before the Rebellion, I believe that the tree was the tree of knowledge of good. The rebellion occurred because God had made man. The great commandment was futuristic. Do you think that Elohim would make a tree grow to cause all of this evil upon the earth? No! Satan poisoned the good fruit with his allegorical DNA.

The soul cannot be altered from what Elohim has made it to be. Regardless of what you do to your body, you are what God has made you. If he made you a woman, you will be a woman for as long as you live. If Elohim made you a man, you will be a man for as long as you shall live. Just because the demon or demons changed your mind to alter your gender, you are still what Elohim made you. The only thing that the demon caused you to do was to be initiated into the realm of eternal damnation.

What was the name of the poison that Satan put into the fruit? What effect did it have on the flesh and mind? It is very apparent that the insane habit of putting something deadly into your mouth has not ceased. Because the flesh was made from the dust of the earth, there are substances from the earth that have an effect on the body. Is there a drug that would cause a rich man to give away all of his money to the poor? Is there a drug that would stop people from killing each other? Is there a substance that will cure the thoughts of evil? No! What I am trying to say is that Satan uses substances to open the doors of your mind and to make the soul helpless. Do you think that a person that is in their right mind would want to kill his or her mother? It is Satan or one of his demons that want you to destroy your mother so that you will die the death of a sinner without hope. The drug epidemic that is in the world is caused by demonic activities. Whatever the substance was that Satan used, it caused Adam and Eve to have uncontrollable lust. This poison of lust is the deadliest thing in existence. There is only one antidote for this poison, and that is the only begotten son of God, Jesus Christ of Nazareth.

Elohim did not give the knowledge of evil to man. Man disobeyed God, and Satan gave it to him. Eve thought that by having this knowledge, she would be like Elohim. Well, there is one thing that is for certain; you do not have to teach anyone how to be evil. A little child's first sign of having the knowledge of evil is the ability to lie. You do not have to go to school to learn how to lie. The only one that can stop you from lying is Elohim, through Jesus Christ, our Lord. Regardless of how good a person may seem to be, that person has the ability to lie. Guess what—Satan is a liar and the father of lying. Modernized evil is the now thing of the devil. The microdemons make people evil without the knowledge of being evil. A gay superstar is not classified as an evil person. A genocidal leader is not considered an evil person, but a hero. A suicide bomber is known as a martyr and is highly honored for killing innocent people. Those who are in great authority uphold the pedophile priests. The river of innocent blood that the genocidal doctors created from killing the unborn is without any remorse. The two-hundred-pound man that is in love with another two-hundred-pound man is without shame. The woman that lusts after another woman is accepted as honorable. The microdemons are in the children for the preparation of totalitarian obedience. Look at the young men and tell me why they wear their pants in such a way that they show their underwear? Why are the young women in hot pursuit for intimacy? Why are the professed preachers becoming adulterous and greedy for filthy lucre? Why did the distinguished mothers start to wear pants, which are not honorable before God? Why did the men decide to wear earrings, which are a sign of femininity in our day? Evil and ungodliness is what Satan and the demons have established as a way of life for this generation. Woe is it unto you for allowing the god of this world to cause you to lose your soul!

For those who are seemingly good, who would not take a dime from someone, who would never commit adultery or fornication, and who (allegorically speaking) would not harm a flea, Satan and the microdemons have developed professional and planned distractions to keep you away from receiving eternal life. The distractions lure men and women away from the conscious fact that they must serve and obey the will of God. Obsession with sports and competitions is one of the distractions that will have an effect on the people on the Day of Judgment. I do not know what shall befall many of the athletes and managers that kept the people from worshipping God on the Lord's Day. I do not know what shall befall the people that own the casinos and the people that play there. All of the people who engage in activities in the world that keep people from worshipping Elohim are at risk of being rebuked. A rebuke from the mouth of Elohim is not good. There was a rebuke from the Lord God a short time ago that resulted in the destruction of a city. Sunday used to be a day that the people in this country honored very highly. The shops and the factories were closed on this day. The custom was that the whole family would dress up and go to the House of God. Now Satan and the demons have distracted the people so greatly that the attendance of games exceeds the number that attends worshipping services. The people used to worship Baal in the olden days. Today, Satan has modernized his technique. Instead of worshipping an image, the people now idolize other people for what they can do with a ball.

The greatest distraction of all is the same one that caused us to be in the state that we are in today. This distraction is the quest for more knowledge than what Elohim has given us. Believe me in what I am about to say. This quest is not always for good, but sometimes for evil. The archeologists dig into the earth for bones and artifacts to try to learn the things of the past, and in so doing, they become foolish, and in many cases, they become fools. The reason Satan gives the archeologists such a great distractive interest in these things is so they will arrive at their conclusive theory, which is that there is no God. By believing this theory, men and women lose their souls. The people have built great museums, the only benefit of which is the display of dead animal bones. Someone living desires a piece of bread just to live. An endangered species has greater rights than an unborn human being. Instead of accepting that which is right, the people are trying to find more ways to become evil.

After Adam and Eve obtained the knowledge of nakedness through disobedience and heard the voice of Elohim while walking in the garden, they thought that they could hide themselves from his presence. Before they heard the voice of Elohim, they sewed fig leaves together to try to cover their shame. The microdemons have caused a reversed sociological reaction. Rather than trying to put on some clothes to cover their shame, the people are doing all that they can to show their shame. Satan and his demons have organized a multi-billion-dollar industry based on man's knowledge of nakedness. The main ingredient of the poison of lust is nakedness. To make my point clear, tell all of the beautiful female movie stars to start dressing like nuns and then see if the men would want to accept them as superstars. You are a star of the devil because of the exposure of your shame and your fictional act of committing adultery and fornication. The reason Elohim did not want Adam and Eve to know the evil of nakedness is that it can cause men and women to lose their souls. Demonic intimate apparel designers design clothes that appeal and attract to generate lust. The intimate publishers publish words and pictures of nakedness for the destruction of pure thoughts. Pornography poisons the mind and can set the stage for every ungodly intimate act among the human race.

The best description of a microdemon infestation is as a house that is vacant, clean, and furnished.

Many people are void of understanding in this world. The people that are without God in their lives are the ones that these demons look for the most. The demons, which have the ability of transferability, alter the mind so they can come and go and do as they please. Allegorically speaking, they have a key to your mind. These demons cause men and women to establish evil and self-destructive habits. When the demons are deceiving somewhere else, a formerly infested person is as normal as anyone is. When the demon or demons do come into that place that they have set up, they cause what they have established to be activated. At a certain time in any evil act, Satan, a demon, or demons are present or have preplanned the event in case of their being absent. To clarify this statement, let us look at some of the devastating habits that are causing great sickness and death. The demons create the thirst for and the addiction to for alcohol. The demons use and cause the prostitutes to lure and destroy the souls of men for gain. When the alcoholic is sober, he or she is normal. When the prostitute is not at her business, she is normal. Satan has done all that he possibly can to make sure that there is not a shortage of things for the destruction of souls. A knife is innocent until a demon uses someone's body to pick it up to murder a human being. A gun is at peace until Satan persuades a person to use it for his causes.

In order to maintain the works of darkness, Satan has set up delusive monetary funds as an incentive for compliance. The incentive for pulling off your clothes before your children and the world is the gain of fame and great riches in this life. To keep the murderous spirit alive, and to generate money to increase evil, the tool of not knowing is utilized. If Satan would make the plot known in the beginning of certain books and movies, he would not be able to use this avenue for his works. Eve was the first human being to be drawn into the Hall of the Unknown. The second human being that was drawn into the Hall of the Unknown was Adam. Ever since then, the whole human race has been addicted to what is not known. Allegorically speaking, Elohim put up a sign that said, "DO NOT ENTER," and because of the generated interest in the unknown, man has summed up his desires in these words, "I must know, regardless of what shall befall me." Many movie stars are drawn into the unknown after the making of a movie. Many of them become intimate without the thought of getting married.

The senses of many people have been poisoned with the desire to know that which is unknown. People are willing to risk their lives just for the sole reason of knowing. In most cases, the adulterer and the adulteress both have clean and honorable spouses. But because of the deceiving demons, men and women are willing to risk a lifetime of joy and happiness for a few minutes of an unknown feeling with someone else. Does the face of another person promote the desire to commit adultery? Does the name of that person create intimate desires? Yes. To experience the unknown is a great deceptive thrill in today's society. Being thrilled unto death is a commonality of many men and women. The propagators spread the knowledge to those that do not know of the many ungodly, intimate acts between the rich and the famous. The propagators are not interested in someone that is poor. There are those that do not want to hear about the suffering of those that are in need. But let a superstar put on a bikini and the world goes crazy.

The works of darkness are about to end. What are you going to do? Are the riches and fame so great that you cannot see? Is this how you value your soul? Have you measured the time of eternal life? Will you continue to forsake the gift of life that Elohim has ordained through his son, Jesus Christ? The demons are going to leave you with their mark for the Second Death. You will not have another opportunity to remove this mark from your soul without repentance.

Chapter Twelve:
The Pseudochurch of the Antichrist and Her Branches

To delude the world regarding his detection, Satan has set up his false churches for operational concealment. I do not want to use the word *church* in this chapter, because there is only one church. However, to pull the cover of concealment off these establishments, I must refer to them as the rejected churches. These rejected churches are where some of the fallen angels hide and work. Satan uses these establishments to fund his operations, to greatly deceive, and to attempt to corrupt the true church of Jesus Christ.

The false sense of salvation in the rejected churches is the main element of deception used by

Satan and the fallen angels. Many people that are in the world have a sincere desire to be saved from the wrath of God and to have a final destination of eternal life in the kingdom of heaven. Satan convinced the fallen angels to follow him into the realm of rejection without any hope whatsoever. He did not use the things and acts that are now in the world, but the words that proceeded out of his mouth. The words that proceeded out of his mouth were the beginning of all of this evil that is now present in the world.

The doctrine for these rejected churches is the doctrine of acknowledgment without repentance. This is why the membership is so great. Mother Mary and the use of the name of Jesus Christ are acknowledged greatly with words and visual manifestations. It is Satan's desire to deceive the whole world. However, to blind the people from detection, he has allowed a few good people to display the characteristics of holiness. I pray that these individuals find grace in the sight of Elohim in the time of need.

There is no salvation in false doctrine. There is also no salvation in the acknowledgment of a name. If the foundation of salvation were based upon acknowledgment, then Jesus Christ would not have had a need to suffer and die for the forgiveness of our sins. Jesus Christ did not come into this world to suffer and die for ours sins that we may continue in them, but that we may condemn the sin that so easily besets us. The deeds of unrighteousness are being committed in these rejected churches because of the said words of Grace, confession, and the works of penitence without the sincere desire to stop sinning. In short, you are at liberty to commit a premeditated sin without being rejected. Those individuals that possess the knowledge of this doctrine have the notion that they will always be forgiven, regardless of what they do. To add fuel to the fire, it is concluded that man cannot live a sinless life after conversion. So according to this philosophy, people are indulging in deadly sins that are not related to breaking the law of the land. The difference between sinners and the members of these rejected churches is that one acknowledges Jesus Christ and the other one does not. The part of committing sin is the same. So if the acknowledgement of Jesus Christ can cause a soul to enter the kingdom of heaven, then why are the preachers preaching so hard? The only thing that a person would have to do would be to make sure that he or she had enough life at the point of death to utter the words, "I believe in the name of Jesus Christ." Baptism is a spiritual, manifested cleansing. If, after the cleansing, you decided to return unto the dirt of sin, then there was no baptism unto repentance. Baptism is for the cleansing of sins to receive a greater baptism, which is from heaven. When you were baptized in the name of the Father and of the Son and of the Holy Ghost, did you receive the gift of the Holy Spirit? The gift of the Holy Spirit gives you the mind and the power to live in a holy manner. If you were baptized in your infancy, then your life should be holy because of the Holy Spirit. If you are sinning against Elohim, then you do not have the Holy Spirit. Faith leads to true repentance, and true repentance leads to true baptism. True baptism leads to the gift of the Holy Spirit. I believed and repented. After I repented, I was baptized in the summational name of the Father, the Son, and the Holy Ghost, which is in the name of Jesus Christ of Nazareth. The reason I was baptized in the name of Jesus Christ of Nazareth is that Pope Stephen was not in existence to receive the mystery of the Gospel. After this true baptism, my life was searched well for an eternal life, and then I was given the Gift of the Holy Spirit. The lives that you are living will declare your true baptisms or your unaccepted baptisms that are not unto repentance.

The present teaching of dogmatism is not unto salvation. Salvation, in its essence, is being freed from sin. When you are given a mind to repent, then salvation has come into the house of your soul. The Gospel of repentance is given to those who start new lives, and not just to those who acknowledge the name of Jesus Christ.

Satan is using you for a shield of concealment. The fallen angels are present among you. They have chosen the establishment of a professed church for protection. Who can get away with felonious acts without being prosecuted? Who can be a reverenced pedophile without going to jail? Who can be a rapist and still be honored among the people? Who can try to change the truth and get a multitude to accept it? God's people are not pedophiles and rapists. God's people do not have the intent to commit sin. God's people strive to improve themselves daily. God's people do not try to change the truth for justification, but they acknowledge that they are wrong when they are wrong. God's people are here for the preparation of the established kingdom of Elohim. Satan is here to try to stop it.

Soon the whole world will be seduced into these rejected churches. Only the Saints, whose names are in the Lamb's Book of Life will be kept from becoming a part of them. Millions will not listen to me. It is your sincere desire to continue in sin. You have become a part of a religion that is without the will to repent.

Many other establishments of concealment do not bear the name of a church. Satan is so cunning that he can use a group of manifested murderers and call it a religion. Satan has devised many lies for his cover. Many organizations use words from the Holy Scriptures for acceptance and recruitment. They have selected words from the Holy Scriptures that are words of acknowledgement, and they have rejected the words that condemn them in their sins. The members in these rejected establishments love ritualism, entertainment, and glorification of historically great individuals. By doing these things, the attention of reality is not focused on them, but is attentive toward the good that someone else has done.

The ritualism of the Old Covenant was used by our schoolmasters to bring us to Christ. The rituals did not cleanse man from sin. The atoning blood of Jesus Christ of Nazareth is the only blood that can cleanse man of his sins. Can a pedophile who has not repented be cleansed of his sins through the Eucharist? No! Can a murderer who has not repented be cleansed of his sins through the Eucharist? No! Is this why the Eucharist is given in every service? The sins of the unrepentant and the taking of the Eucharist can cause death. The Eucharist is for those who have repented of their sins with the sincere desire to never commit them again. The only creature that would tell you that you could take part in the Eucharist without repentance is the devil.

Ritualism and religious artifacts are being used to destroy the consciousness of sin. What is confession without repentance? If you are committing fornication with the intent of never stopping, then what is confession? If you murdered someone yesterday and you have the intent to murder someone tomorrow, what is confession? It is written: "if we confess our sin, he is faithful and just to forgive us of our sins." To be forgiven, you must have the confessed will to stop.

Satan's businesses are intended to deceive people to keep as many souls as possible out of the kingdom of God. People love to hear the benefits of being a part of an organization that will guarantee them eternal life. It is not about dogmatism! It is about the truth! Someone has put a word pacifier into your mouth to keep you from finding out the truth. God sent his son, Jesus Christ of Nazareth, into the world to save his people from their sins. Tell your leader to tell you the truth that you might be saved from the wrath of God! Satan is deceiving millions of souls into eternal damnation because of the philosophy of verbal acknowledgements. Satan will bring his dominant, evil works into existence through occultism. Which establishment will he use? Will he start out in a small group? Where will the Antichrist get the money to become an international leader within a very short time? Are the weapons and all of the high-tech equipment that are being made going to be used for his cause of totalitarian authority? The False Prophet will soon create a lying wonder to recruit the world into this known order. Do you think that Satan will start his totalitarian ruling in the future, or did he start working on it almost two thousand years ago? The Antichrist will incorporate every deceived nation under heaven for his false deification ceremony. His person of embodiment will sit in the temple at Jerusalem to fulfill the abomination of desolation. He will establish the mark for the international acceptance of his order. Everyone that is not of his order will suffer. The key to death will be given to all of those who will not comply.

Shame on you, nations of sin. Shame on you, all you deceived dignitaries. The path of light was ever before you, but you chose the path of darkness. Your souls are now without hope, and you have been excluded from the blessing of eternal life.

Shall I write more to you than what I have already written? Will you listen? I think not! Your DNA has been poisoned beyond repair! Your sins and abominations have opened a great portal for the Antichrist to enter that he may begin the use of his time allotment for totalitarian ruling.

CONCLUSION

Are the three books that I have written a part of vanity? Can these words stop what is about to take place? Noah preached for many years, and only he and his family were saved from the Great Flood. This generation has the same lack of understanding as those before the flood, which is exemplified by the allegorical saying, "I will believe it when I see it." The knowledge of the Seventh Sense is too great to be revealed to this wicked generation. But I will say this: "Tomorrow is already finished." What is your defense, and where is your safety? If you decided to try to rebuild the Tower of Babel to heaven, it would be in vain. If you decided to try to dig unto the foundation of the earth and lay another one, you still would be hopeless. Your weapons are laced with sin, and your council is for abominations. Fall is at your doorstep, and Rise has ended her stay. Your soldiers and your weapons are useless, because your enemies sin and abomination are embodied within. Can whoremongers and whores fight in a war against evil? Can gays and lesbians fight in a war against evil? Can a nation fight in a war against evil when sins and abominations are upheld?

You removed your defenses from their foundation that sins and abominations might have a free course. The Man of Sin shall rise in the East, and the West shall be darkened. Prayers are not answered without repentance. The secularists and the evolutionists are full of the cancer cells of reprobation. There is a great mystery concerning repentance. Mercy is granted even if you will repent in the future. God allows you the time to fulfill the act of repentance. When you see the judgments of God's hand upon people, you know that their repentance was not seen through the eyes of our omniscient God. The wrath of Elohim can and has brought man back into a repentant state.

Can the great weapons that you now have keep you from falling? You allowed Satan to counsel you and allow you to come into his regime. His goal is the embodiment of deification in the temple at Jerusalem. If you show signs of resistance, he will be merciless upon that nation.

It is sad to say this, but there is a great nation that will be destroyed from within. The reason the apostle John used the allegorical name Mystery Babylon the Great was to preserve the mystery thereof until the time of fulfillment. She now bears a manifested name. Moreover, the sinners can see her futuristic fall, and the unrighteous can witness her sufferings!

If you would only listen to me, we might have a few more good years together. Elohim has brought us through so much! From the beginning to this very day, hope has always been there for us! Now the people are looking to the foolish ones for hope. There is only one hope, and anything else is delusive.

You do not want the words of life to exist in your council. You do not want to see the remembrance of his suffering for you on your badges. You do not want to give him reverence for security and safety. You are so evil that you have populated your desires so that many will do likewise.

Satan's wishes are now in place. The shield of faith has been removed from before and placed behind. The Sword of the Spirit has been muzzled by the council that the ideology of demons might have a voice. The truth that held up your dignity has been rejected for lies! The breastplate of righteousness has been replaced with the thin cloth of sin. The helmet of salvation was taken off and put into a museum.

Oh nation that bears a mysterious name, Satan has sedated you with the poison of lust and made you naked. He has made you naked so that his fiery darts may pierce you and draw you into his realm of hopelessness. Amen.

Chapter: Past Conclusion
A Touch of the
Seventh Sense

Why are we here? What is the purpose of my existence? We have seen the beginning of a people that will not grieve Elohim. The day of a day that no human has ever seen or witnessed is near. The Lord our God has prepared a new world for the saints, whom he has greatly blessed. The six senses that we now have cannot comprehend the future. The six senses are for the one faith that God has established with his people. The eyes that we have can only see the things that Elohim has made for faith.

Between the end of the first beginning to the beginning of the last beginning, Elohim created a new heaven and a new earth. There was no sea. The city that Elohim made was manifested. The gates were opened, and the people rejoiced. The judgment of the righteous was for good. The bodies for the Saints are possessed. The poison of lust is no more. The Saints have eaten from the Tree of Life. The day that will never end has begun. Evil has been destroyed. The gift of the Holy Spirit is the beginning of immortality.

The mystery of OMNISCIENT BEFORE, OMNISCIENT AFTER, OMNISCIENT CHANGE, and OMNISCIENT ACCEPTANCE can only be fully understood by the seventh sense. What Elohim has ordained and allowed to exist cannot be changed. I have never seen a man or any other creature make something from nothing. Elohim made everything that our senses have experienced from the beginning. Elohim provided the substances and the knowledge to form, from the earth, many of the visible things we now see.

OMNISCIENT BEFORE cannot be changed! The Word of God has declared a day of judgment, and no one can stop it from existing! OMNISCIENT AFTER went forth into the future and awaits the time of fulfillment. OMNISCIENT CHANGE fixed the words that the prophets spoke so that nothing in existence could alter or change them. OMNISCIENT ACCEPTANCE brought OMNISCIENT BEFORE, OMNISCIENT AFTER, and OMNISCIENT CHANGE to the Elect of Elohim and rested upon them.

My works, which Elohim has ordained for me, were already finished before I was born. It is impossible to change the omniscient foreknowledge of Elohim. Someone can speak to Elohim on our behalf, and that someone is Christ Jesus our Lord. Elohim, who is the owner of OMNISCIENT BEFORE, OMNISCIENT AFTER, OMNISCIENT CHANGE, and OMNISCIENT ACCEPTANCE , can do as he pleases.